CONTENTS

Toby Twirl and the Reindeer

Toby Twirl and Friends Stickers

Game: Potato Race

Game: Let Us All Go Sledging

Sticker Landscape

Pictures for you to Colour

ISBN 978-0-9544720-1-6
All Rights Reserved. Designated trademarks, illustrations and brands are the exclusive property and Copyright of Toby Twirl Ltd © 2007

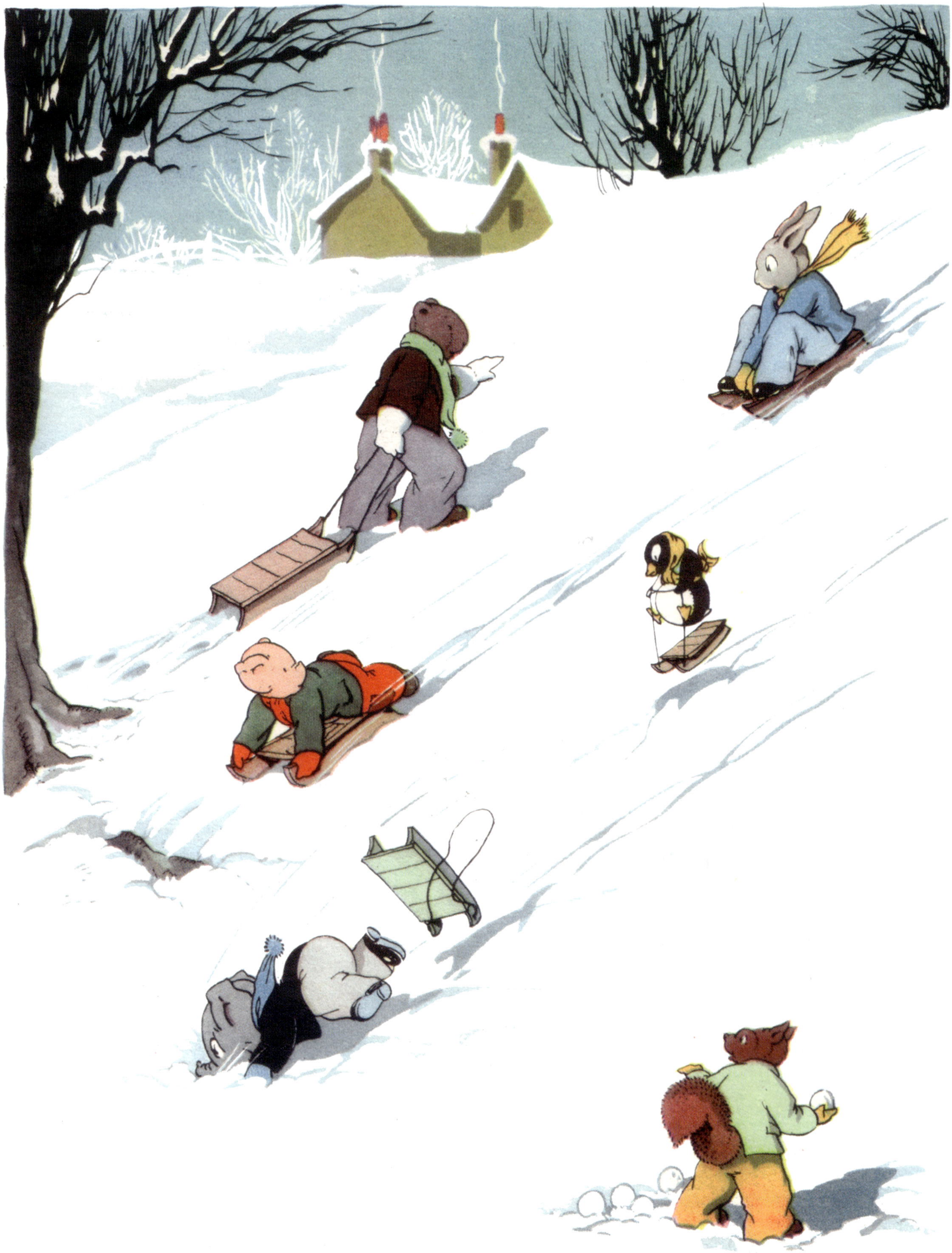

Toby Twirl and the Reindeer

One day, just before Christmas, Toby and his friends decided to go tobogganing. They all met in the Village Square, warmly wrapped in thick coats and scarves and pulling their toboggans behind them. "I know a wonderful place for tobogganing", said Eli. "Well, show us the way then," shouted the others, and so, led by Eli, they all tramped away. They very soon reached the hill that Eli knew and climbed right up to the top. Then one by one they clambered onto their toboggans and away they raced to the bottom of the hill. Once or twice somebody tumbled off, but nobody was hurt, and so with a lot of laughing and teasing, they picked themselves up and climbed to the top of the hill again.

Faster and faster they went as the track hardened into ice, until the downward ride was very exciting indeed. After a while, as they all sat at the top of the hill, resting after the steep climb upwards, they heard footsteps, and turning round, to their amazement saw that Father Christmas was walking towards them. "Hello Children", he called out, smiling in a kindly way at them, "I wonder if you could help me. My Reindeer has gone lame with a stone in his hoof, and I can't get it out".

"Why yes," said Toby excitedly, "we can take him to the village blacksmith's for you." "That's right," all the others cried, "so we can." "Good lads." said Father Christmas, "I thought you might be able to help."

So down the other side of the hill they followed Father Christmas until they came to a Sleigh. They saw that the Reindeer, which was harnessed to it, was holding one foot up as though it hurt him to put it to the ground.

"Poor old thing," cried Toby, "we'll soon have that taken out for you."

They helped Father Christmas to un-harness him, and then a halter was placed round his neck.

"I'll wait here," he said, "for I am tired and could do with forty winks." Father Christmas climbed into the Sleigh and covered himself with a rug.

"We shan't be long," they cried, as slowly they led the Reindeer away.
The poor thing could only use three of it's feet, so was only able to hobble along.

At last they reached the village, and watched curiously by everybody, they led the Reindeer to the Blacksmith's Forge.

"Whatever have you got there, lads?" asked the Blacksmith, as he came out of the Forge, wiping his big hands on his leather apron. "A Reindeer, eh? What do you want, a new set of antlers for it? Ha! Ha! Ha!"

"No," said Toby, when they had all finished laughing at the Blacksmith's joke, "we want you to get a stone out of his hoof."

"Bring him in then," said the Blacksmith, so the friends led the Reindeer into the Forge.

"Aye, it's stuck pretty fast," he said, as he struggled to get it out. "Mmm! Ah! That's got it," he cried, and held up the stone for them to see. Then he bathed the sore hoof and put some ointment on it. "There, that'll do," he said with a smile. "He'd even pull Father Christmas from Toyland now."

"He's got to," said Pete solemnly, "for he belongs to Father Christmas." "Ho! ho! ho! ha! ha! ha!" roared the Blacksmith. "Oh dear, Father Christmas's Reindeer. Haw! haw! haw!"

So leaving the Blacksmith, still holding his sides and roaring with laughter at what he thought was a huge joke, they led the Reindeer back to the Sleigh.

They woke Father Christmas who was fast asleep, and he jumped up at once. "Good work, my lads," he cried, "you deserve a reward for your kindness." He scratched his head, and then slapped his thigh. "And by golly," he shouted, "you shall have one. Come on help me harness this Reindeer."

They did as they were told and then he told them to jump onto the Sleigh. In high excitement they all tumbled on, and then with a merry word, Father Christmas bade the Reindeer start.

As they sped along in the Sleigh, Father Christmas burst into song, and very soon the others followed him until they were all singing at the top of their voices. They did have a jolly time, carol after carol they sang, until Father Christmas suddenly stopped.

"Here we are," he cried, "you are now in Santa Claus's Toyland," Hurriedly they climbed out of the Sleigh and looked around them.

Everything they could see was a toy. They hurried into a big doll's house where a lot of elves and fairies were busily packing up parcels.

They all looked up and smiled when they saw Father Christmas, and one fairy hurried up to speak to him. "We shall be ready just in time," she said, "we've had such a rush this year."

"Good, good," cried Father Christmas, "well done. It's a busy time for all of us, eh?" The fairy smiled and hurried away again. Meanwhile Toby and the others had been looking round in great excitement, for all around them they could see the most beautiful toys.

"Now then," said Father Christmas merrily, turning to them again, "in return for your kindness to me, I shall let you all choose your own present this year. So just wander round and see what you would like the most. Just anything at all that is here."

"Anything?" gasped Toby. Father Christmas nodded and hurried over to a fairy who was beckoning him. So the friends walked round looking at all the wonderful toys they could see.

"Well?" asked Father Christmas, coming up to them a little later, "have you decided what you want?" "Yes please," cried Pete, nearly falling over in excitement. "I'd like that great big trumpet up there." They all laughed when they saw what Pete had chosen, but Father Christmas nodded his head and took out a little book. "Peter Penguin, a big trumpet," he wrote. "And I'd like that lovely yacht," cried Eli eagerly. "Please may I have that beautiful fort with all the soldiers on it?" asked Toby. And so Father Christmas wrote down what each of them wanted. A scooter for Ben Beaver, and a bright red hoop for Harold Hare. "And now you must go home," he said when he had done, "or your mothers will be wondering where you are." So out into the snow he led them, and once more they all clambered onto the Sleigh and away they flew. Father Christmas took them to where they had left their toboggans, then with a wave of his hand he sped away.

They all hurried home, talking and chattering in high excitement. They could hardly wait for Christmas Day to come. But at last it did come, and sure enough when each of them woke up, they found the toy they had asked for at the bottom of their beds. They were lucky, weren't they ?

Toby & Friends Sticker Page

You can use some of these on the sticker landscape page

Potato Race - a Game for you to play

POTATO RACE - A scoring game for 2 to 4 players

You require five small buttons to represent potatoes for each track, a coloured counter or button for each player and a dice for scoring. To begin, the players choose a colour and line up opposite No 1 on the track corresponding to their colour. Then throw the dice in turn and move forward the number indicated. A six does not entitle you to an extra throw. The exact number must be thrown to enable a player to collect one potato. When the correct number is thrown, the player collects one potato and returns to their No 1 position ready to play again in turn. Play continues until one player becomes the first to collect all five potatoes.

LET US ALL GO SLEDGING!

Now are we all ready? – If you throw six with the dice you can go off on this fun toboggan run to Nanna Beaver's Tuck Shop. Use coloured buttons or counters and don't forget you must throw the exact amount with the dice to get into Nanna's Tuck Shop - but watch how you go - there are some very tricky spots on this run!

STEEP HILL-GO FORWARD TO 10 - 1 MOVE FOR EACH TURN

QUICK RUN DOWN TO 21

IT'S A LOVELY SWITCHBACK NOW – ZOOM FORWARD TO 120

SLEDGE OVERTURNS MISS 1 TURN

HERE'S A LOVELY BEND - SWING ON TO 98

CINDERS ON ROAD MISS 2 TURNS TO SWEEP UP

TAKE SHORT CUT TO 99

ROAD COVERED WITH ICE SHOOT ON TO 96

BUMP IN TO TREE - GO BACK TO 73 FOR REPAIRS

SLIP AND SLIDE DOWN HILL TO 24
EASY CLIMB - RUN ON TO 38
GRAND RUN DOWN HERE GO ON TO 53 - BUT MIND THE BEND!
OUT OF BREATH - WAIT 2 TURNS
YOU ARE IN DITCH MISS 2 TURNS
YOU ARE DOING FINE - GO ON TO 78
RUNNER OFF SLEDGE GO TO BLACKSMITH AT 73
NANNA BEAVER'S TUCK SHOP
COLLISION AT CROSS ROADS - GO BACK TO START
GOOD GOING HERE SWING ALONG TO 126
YOU ARE OFF THE ROAD INTO A POND - GO BACK TO 73 AND DRY YOUR CLOTHES
COLLISION AT CROSS ROADS GO BACK TO START
THIS WAY
28
29
30
31
32
33
34
35
36
37
38
39
40
41
42
43
44
45
46
47
48
49
50
51
52
53
54
55
56
57
58
59
60
61
62
63
64
65
66
67
68
69
70
71
72
106
107
108
109
110
111
112
113
114
115
116
117
118
119
120
121
122
123
124
125
126
127
128
129
130

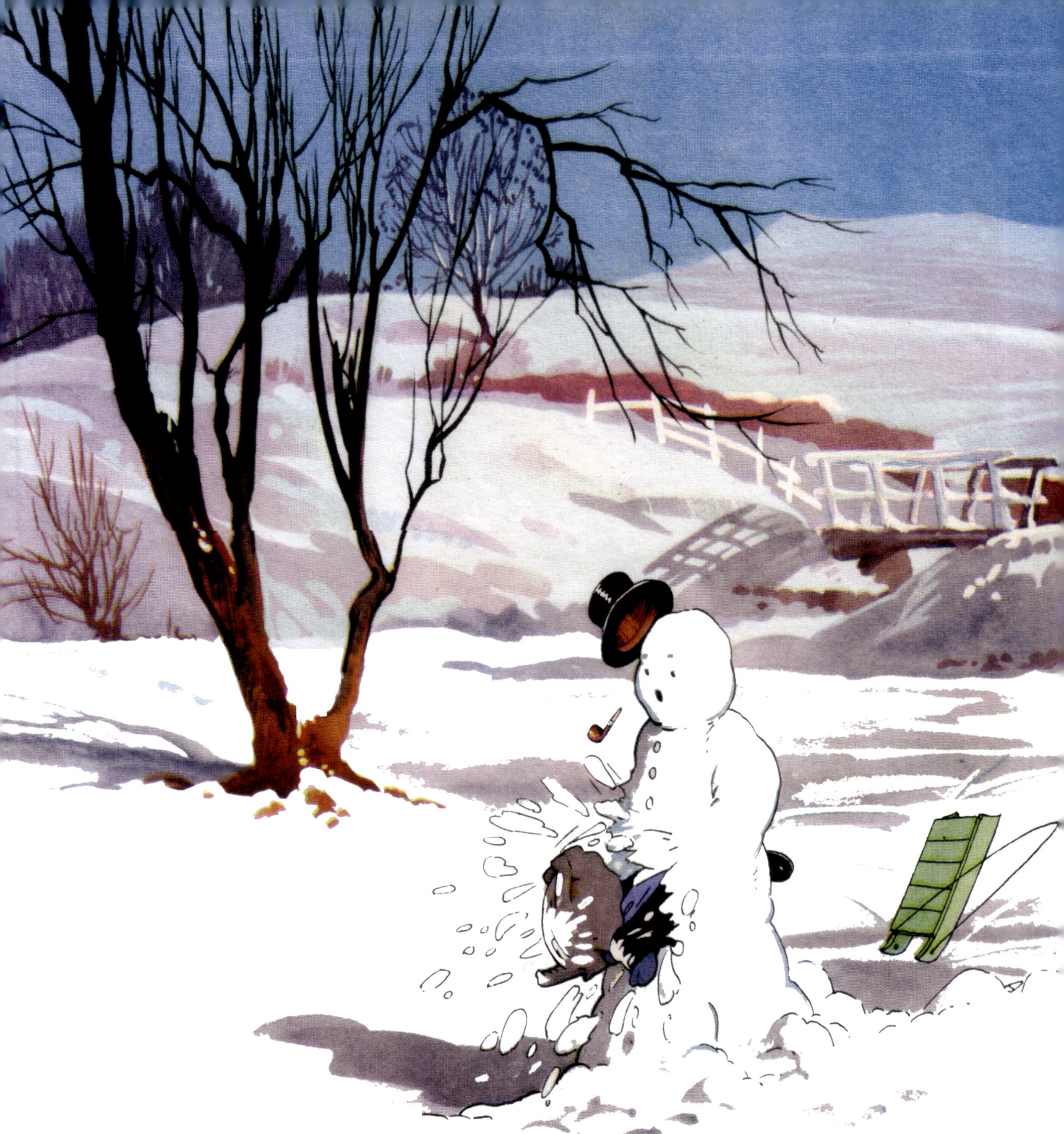

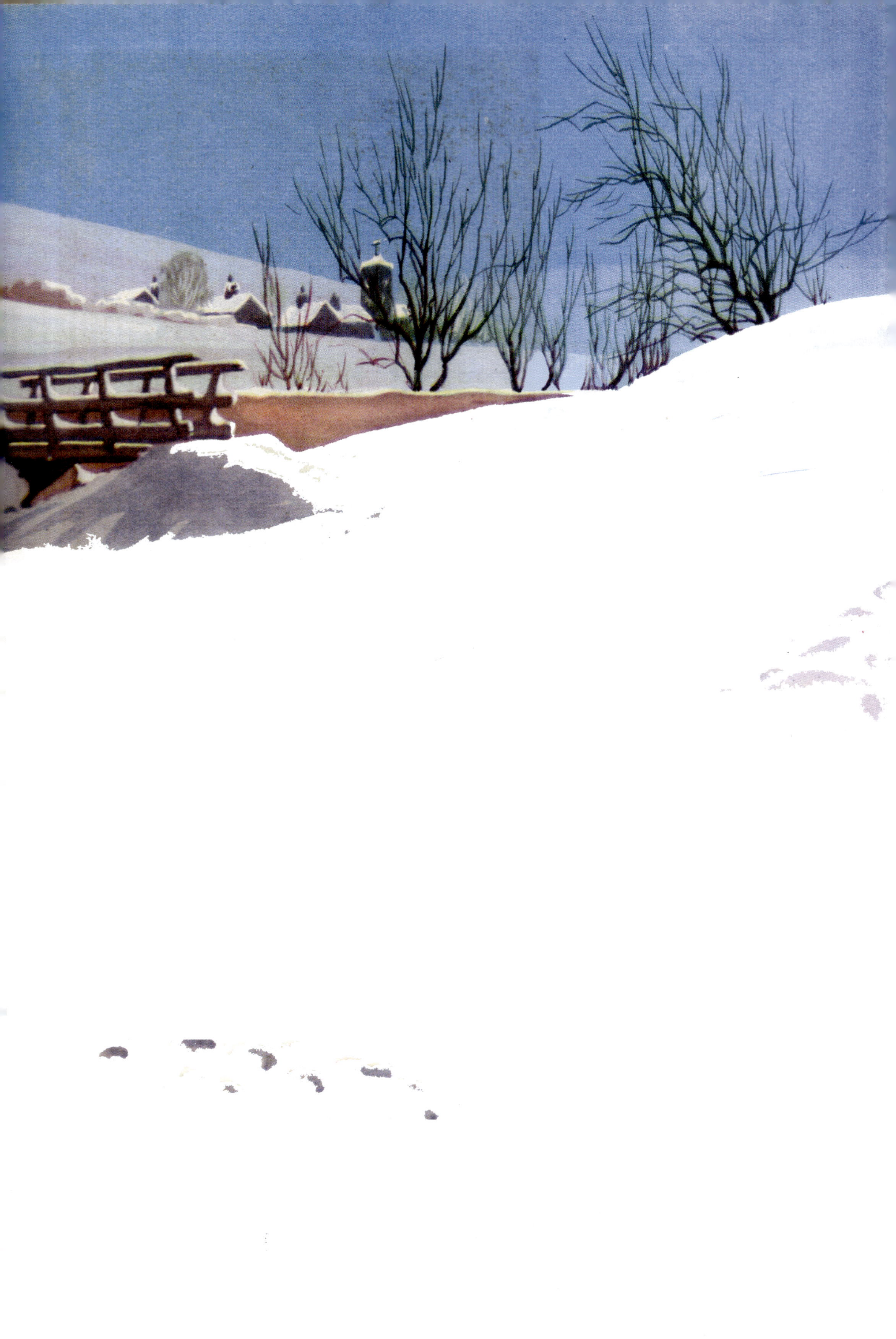

A Picture for you to colour !

Here is your colour guide:

Lots of Fun in the Snow

A Picture for you to colour !

Here is your colour guide:

Toby and Friends have built a Snow Man!

A Picture for you to colour !

Here is your colour guide:

Toby and Friends Ride on Santa's Sleigh